The Power of Living Slow

Find Joy and Satisfaction in the Present Moment

Aiken Carlson

The Power of Living Slow

Table of Contents

Chapter 1: Redefining Success and Time

Challenging Conventional Notions of Success

The notion of success has long been defined by societal benchmarks—wealth, status, career achievements, and the accumulation of material possessions. These measures, however, often overlook the nuances and individual preferences that truly define a fulfilling life. The conventional idea of success is deeply rooted in our education systems, media portrayals, and cultural narratives, which all emphasize the pursuit of external validation and tangible accomplishments. Yet, there is a growing recognition that these traditional yardsticks may not align with personal happiness or well-being.

The journey to question and redefine success begins with introspection. It requires peeling back layers of societal conditioning to uncover what genuinely resonates with one's values and desires. This process entails a conscious effort to detach from the expectations imposed by peers, family, and society at large. By doing so, individuals can begin to craft a personal definition of success that is aligned with their unique aspirations and circumstances.

One major aspect of this redefinition involves the relationship between success and time. In the modern world, time is often equated with money, leading to a relentless cycle of productivity and efficiency. However, this mindset can result in burnout and a diminished quality of life. By challenging the conventional notion that success must be achieved swiftly and at all costs, individuals can embrace a more deliberate approach to time. This means valuing experiences over achievements, and understanding that a slower pace can foster deeper satisfaction and contentment.

Furthermore, the relationship between success and happiness is complex and often misunderstood. While it is easy to assume that success leads to happiness, the reality is that the pursuit of success can sometimes lead to stress and dissatisfaction. This paradox arises because traditional success metrics are often external and do not account for the intrinsic elements that contribute to happiness, such as meaningful relationships, personal growth, and a sense of purpose. By prioritizing these internal aspects, individuals can cultivate a sense of fulfillment that transcends conventional success.

Prioritizing what truly matters is a pivotal step in this transformative journey. It requires a shift in focus from external achievements to the cultivation of inner values and passions. This may involve reevaluating career paths, lifestyle choices, and personal commitments to ensure they align with one's authentic self. By doing so, individuals can create a balanced life that reflects their truest desires and aspirations.

Creating balance is not merely about managing time or juggling responsibilities. It involves a holistic approach to life, where various aspects such as health, relationships, and personal interests are integrated harmoniously. This balance allows individuals to thrive in multiple dimensions, rather than excelling in one area at the expense of others. By fostering equilibrium, individuals can experience a richer, more nuanced understanding of success that encompasses all facets of life.

Patience plays a crucial role in personal growth and the redefinition of success. In a culture that prizes instant gratification, cultivating patience can be a powerful antidote to the pressures of conventional success. Embracing patience means recognizing that true growth and achievement often require time, persistence, and resilience. It is about understanding that setbacks and challenges are integral to the journey and that lasting success is built on a foundation of perseverance and learning.

This approach to success is not about rejecting ambition or the pursuit of goals. Rather, it is about ensuring that these pursuits are aligned with one's core values and contribute to overall well-being. It involves setting meaningful goals that reflect personal aspirations, rather than those dictated by external standards. By doing so, individuals can pursue success on their own terms, free from the constraints of societal expectations.

Ultimately, challenging conventional notions of success is an empowering process that allows individuals to forge a path that is uniquely their own. It is about embracing authenticity, creativity, and individuality in the pursuit of a life that is rich in meaning and fulfillment. This journey requires courage and self-awareness, but the rewards are profound—a deeper sense of purpose, a greater appreciation for the present moment, and a more holistic understanding of what it means to truly succeed.

In redefining success, individuals can also inspire others to question and reassess their own beliefs and values. By living authentically and prioritizing what truly matters, they become role models for a more sustainable and fulfilling way of life. This ripple effect can lead to broader societal change, as more people adopt a more holistic and personalized approach to success.

The journey to redefine success is deeply personal and ongoing. It involves a constant process of reflection and adjustment, as individuals navigate the complexities of modern life. It requires an openness to change and a willingness to challenge long-held beliefs. Yet, through this process, individuals can discover a more profound and lasting form of success—one that is rooted in genuine happiness, personal fulfillment, and a deep connection to oneself and the world around them.

The Relationship Between Time and Happiness

Time, in its relentless march, often dictates the rhythm of our lives. The relationship between time and happiness is a complex and intricate dance, where perceptions of time can significantly influence our well-being. In modern society, where the pace of life seems to quicken with each passing day, understanding this relationship is crucial for nurturing a more content and fulfilled existence.

The concept of time has evolved alongside human civilization. Ancient cultures revered time as a cyclical force, one that governed the natural world and the lives within it. The rhythms of the sun, moon, and seasons were intricately woven into daily life. However, with the advent of industrialization and the rise of the clock, time became linear and segmented. This shift brought about a new urgency, a compulsion to maximize productivity and efficiency, often at the expense of individual well-being.

The relentless pursuit of time efficiency has given rise to a culture where busyness is often equated with success. People find themselves trapped in an unending cycle of work and obligations, leaving little room for leisure or relaxation. This frenetic pace can lead to a sense of time poverty, where individuals feel they never have enough hours in the day to accomplish their tasks or enjoy life. The pressure to constantly do more can lead to stress, burnout, and a diminished quality of life.

Conversely, when individuals perceive they have ample time, they experience a greater sense of control and autonomy. This perception fosters a feeling of abundance, where life is not dictated by the clock but by personal choice and preference. When people have the freedom to choose how they spend their time, they are more likely to engage in activities that bring joy and fulfillment. This sense of agency is a key component of happiness, as it empowers individuals to live in alignment with their values and aspirations.

The relationship between time and happiness is further influenced by the concept of presence. Being fully present in the moment allows individuals to savor experiences and deepen their appreciation for life. It involves a conscious effort to let go of distractions and focus on the here and now. This mindfulness can transform ordinary experiences into moments of joy and connection, enhancing the overall quality of life. The practice of presence encourages individuals to slow down, to relish simple pleasures, and to cultivate gratitude for the present moment.

The perception of time can also affect how individuals form and maintain relationships. Quality time spent with loved ones fosters intimacy and connection, strengthening the bonds that contribute to a sense of belonging and happiness. In a world where digital communication often replaces face-to-face interaction, prioritizing time for meaningful connections can be a powerful antidote to loneliness and isolation. By dedicating time to nurture relationships, individuals can create a supportive network that enriches their lives and enhances their well-being.

The ability to manage time effectively is another vital aspect of the time-happiness equation. Time management is not merely about scheduling tasks or maximizing productivity; it involves prioritizing activities that align with one's values and goals. By focusing on what truly matters, individuals can create a balanced life that fosters personal growth and satisfaction. This intentional approach to time management allows individuals to allocate their energy and resources to pursuits that contribute to their overall happiness.

Moreover, the relationship between time and happiness extends to the way individuals perceive the passage of time. The perception of time as fleeting or abundant can shape one's outlook on life. Those who view time as fleeting may live with a sense of urgency, constantly racing against the clock. Conversely, those who perceive time as abundant may adopt a more relaxed and contented approach to life. Cultivating a mindset that embraces the passage of time as a natural and inevitable process can lead to greater acceptance and peace.

The relationship between time and happiness is also evident in the way individuals set and pursue goals. Goals provide a sense of direction and purpose, guiding individuals toward a desired outcome. However, the pursuit of goals should not come at the expense of the present moment. Balancing future aspirations with present enjoyment is essential for maintaining a sense of happiness and fulfillment. By setting realistic and meaningful goals, individuals can create a roadmap for their lives that aligns with their values and passions.

Ultimately, the relationship between time and happiness is deeply personal and unique to each individual. It requires an ongoing exploration of one's values, priorities, and aspirations. By understanding the intricate dance between time and happiness, individuals can make intentional choices that enhance their well-being and enrich their lives. This journey involves embracing the present moment, prioritizing meaningful connections, and aligning one's life with personal values and goals. Through this process, individuals can cultivate a deeper sense of happiness and fulfillment, one that transcends the constraints of time and resonates with the essence of who they are.

Prioritizing What Truly Matters

In an era where distractions abound and the noise of daily life can easily overwhelm, prioritizing what truly matters has become an essential skill. Our lives are often cluttered with obligations, demands, and the relentless pursuit of goals that may not align with our deepest values. Yet, beneath this cacophony lies the potential for a life that resonates with authenticity and purpose, a life where we focus on what genuinely holds significance to us.

The first step in this journey is self-reflection. It requires pausing amidst the hustle and bustle to ask ourselves fundamental questions: What brings us joy? What are our core values? What do we want to be remembered for? These inquiries guide us toward understanding what genuinely matters and help us discern between essential pursuits and mere distractions. By identifying our true priorities, we can begin to align our actions with our innermost desires.

Once we have clarity on what matters most, the challenge becomes integrating these priorities into our daily lives. This often requires making conscious choices about how we spend our time and energy. It involves setting boundaries and learning to say no to activities and commitments that do not serve our greater purpose. By doing so, we create space for the things that truly enrich our lives, whether that be nurturing relationships, pursuing creative passions, or engaging in activities that bring us peace and fulfillment.

One effective strategy for prioritizing what matters is the practice of intentional living. This involves making deliberate choices that reflect our values and goals, rather than allowing external pressures to dictate our actions. Intentional living encourages us to be present and mindful in each moment, to savor our experiences, and to cultivate gratitude for the simple pleasures in life. By living with intention, we can create a life that feels meaningful and aligned with our true selves.

Another important aspect of prioritizing what matters is the willingness to embrace change. As we grow and evolve, our priorities may shift, and what once seemed crucial may no longer hold the same significance. It is essential to remain flexible and open to reevaluating our values and goals as we navigate the complexities of life. This adaptability allows us to stay true to ourselves and ensures that our actions remain aligned with what truly matters.

Cultivating meaningful relationships is often at the heart of what matters most to individuals. Humans are inherently social beings, and our connections with others play a vital role in our overall well-being. Prioritizing time for family, friends, and loved ones can provide a sense of belonging and support that is invaluable in our journey toward fulfillment. By investing in these relationships, we create a network of love and connection that enriches our lives and provides a foundation for happiness.

In addition to nurturing relationships, it is important to prioritize self-care and personal well-being. Taking care of our physical, emotional, and mental health is crucial for living a balanced and fulfilling life. This may involve setting aside time for activities that recharge and rejuvenate us, such as exercise, meditation, or hobbies that bring us joy. By prioritizing self-care, we ensure that we have the energy and resilience to pursue what truly matters.

The process of prioritizing what matters also involves letting go of the need for perfection and embracing imperfection as a natural part of life. The pursuit of perfection can lead to stress and dissatisfaction, diverting our attention from the things that genuinely matter. By accepting our imperfections and embracing the beauty of imperfection in others, we create a more compassionate and forgiving outlook on life. This acceptance allows us to focus on what is truly important, rather than getting caught up in unrealistic expectations.

It is also valuable to consider the impact of our choices on the broader world. Prioritizing what matters may involve making conscious decisions to live sustainably and ethically, ensuring that our actions align with our values and contribute positively to the community and environment. This sense of responsibility and awareness can deepen our connection to the world around us and enhance our sense of purpose.

Ultimately, prioritizing what truly matters is an ongoing journey, one that requires continuous reflection, intention, and adaptation. It is about creating a life that is rich in meaning and aligned with our deepest values, a life that allows us to live authentically and wholeheartedly. By focusing on what truly matters, we can cultivate a sense of fulfillment and joy that transcends the noise of everyday life and resonates with the essence of who we are.

Creating a Balanced Life

The quest for balance in life often feels like walking a tightrope, where even a slight misstep can tip the scales. In a world that constantly demands more of our time and energy, creating a balanced life is both a challenge and a necessity. It is about orchestrating the various components of our existence—work, relationships, health, and personal growth—into a harmonious symphony that resonates with our values and aspirations.

Achieving balance begins with an honest assessment of how we currently allocate our time and energy. Many of us find ourselves caught in a whirlwind of commitments, obligations, and expectations. This frenetic pace can leave us feeling overwhelmed and disconnected from our true selves. To regain balance, it's imperative to take a step back and evaluate the areas of our lives that require more attention, as well as those that may be consuming more than their fair share of our resources.

Once we have identified the areas that need adjustment, the next step is to establish clear priorities. This involves distinguishing between what is urgent and what is truly important. Urgent tasks often create a false sense of importance, pulling us away from activities that genuinely contribute to our well-being. By focusing on what truly matters, we can allocate our time and energy more effectively, ensuring that we are nurturing all aspects of our lives.

Creating a balanced life also requires setting boundaries. In a culture that often equates busyness with success, it can be difficult to say no to additional responsibilities or commitments. However, setting boundaries is essential for protecting our time and energy. It allows us to create space for the things that bring us joy and fulfillment, rather than being constantly pulled in multiple directions. Establishing boundaries involves clear communication with others about our limits and needs, as well as being mindful of our own capacity.

Another key component of a balanced life is the integration of self-care. Taking care of our physical, mental, and emotional health is foundational to maintaining balance. This means prioritizing activities that recharge and rejuvenate us, such as exercise, meditation, or pursuits that bring us pleasure. Self-care is not a luxury; it is a necessity. By investing in our well-being, we build the resilience and energy needed to meet the demands of daily life.

Mindfulness plays a significant role in creating balance, as it encourages us to be present in each moment. When we practice mindfulness, we become more aware of our thoughts, emotions, and actions, allowing us to respond to life's challenges with greater clarity and intention. Mindfulness helps us to slow down, to appreciate the beauty in the ordinary, and to cultivate a sense of gratitude for the present moment. This awareness can lead to more thoughtful decision-making and a deeper connection to ourselves and others.

In addition to mindfulness, cultivating a balanced life involves finding joy in the journey, rather than fixating solely on outcomes. Life is not a linear path, and the pursuit of balance requires flexibility and adaptability. Embracing the ebb and flow of life allows us to navigate challenges with grace and resilience. It is about finding contentment in the present, even amidst the chaos, and recognizing that balance is a dynamic state, one that requires continuous adjustment and recalibration.

Relationships are a vital aspect of a balanced life, providing support, connection, and meaning. Nurturing our relationships with family, friends, and loved ones is essential for our well-being. This means dedicating time to cultivate these connections, engaging in meaningful conversations, and being present for one another. Strong relationships create a sense of belonging and community, offering a foundation of love and support that enriches our lives.

Creating balance also involves aligning our actions with our values and goals. It is about living authentically and ensuring that our daily choices reflect our true selves. This alignment fosters a sense of purpose and fulfillment, allowing us to pursue our passions and aspirations with intention. By staying true to our values, we can create a life that feels meaningful and aligned with our inner compass.

Lastly, it is important to recognize that balance is not about perfection. It is a fluid and ever-changing process that requires patience and self-compassion. There will be times when one area of life demands more attention, and that's okay. The key is to remain flexible and open to change, adjusting our priorities and actions as needed. By embracing this dynamic approach to balance, we can create a life that is rich in meaning, harmony, and joy.

In the end, creating a balanced life is about weaving together the various threads of our existence into a cohesive tapestry. It is a journey of self-discovery, where we learn to navigate the complexities of life with intention and grace. By prioritizing what truly matters, setting boundaries, and nurturing our well-being, we can cultivate a life that is both fulfilling and balanced. This harmony allows us to live authentically, with a deep sense of purpose and connection to ourselves and the world around us.

The Role of Patience in Personal Growth

Patience, often seen as a passive virtue, is in fact a powerful catalyst for personal growth. In a world that prizes immediacy and quick results, cultivating patience can provide a profound shift in perspective, offering individuals the ability to embrace the journey of personal development with grace and resilience. It is through patience that we learn to navigate life's complexities, face challenges with equanimity, and allow ourselves the time to evolve into our best selves.

At its core, patience is the capacity to accept or tolerate delay, difficulty, or discomfort without becoming agitated or upset. It is an active process that requires conscious effort and practice. Embracing patience begins with the recognition that growth is not a linear path but a journey filled with twists and turns. This journey is marked by moments of progress and setbacks, each contributing to the tapestry of our personal development. By understanding that growth takes time, we can cultivate a mindset that values long-term progress over immediate gratification.

One of the key aspects of patience in personal growth is the ability to remain present and engaged in the process, even when the outcomes are uncertain. This involves letting go of the need for immediate results and embracing the unfolding of our experiences. Patience allows us to remain open to learning and growth, even in the face of adversity. It encourages us to view challenges as opportunities for development, rather than obstacles to be avoided. By adopting this perspective, we can transform setbacks into stepping stones on our journey toward self-improvement.

In the pursuit of personal growth, patience also plays a crucial role in fostering self-compassion. Often, we are our harshest critics, setting unrealistic expectations for ourselves and becoming frustrated when we fall short. Patience invites us to extend the same kindness and understanding to ourselves that we would offer to a friend. It reminds us that growth is a gradual process and that it is okay to make mistakes along the way. By practicing self-compassion, we create a supportive environment for our personal development, allowing us to learn from our experiences without judgment.

Moreover, patience is essential in the cultivation of meaningful relationships, which are integral to personal growth. Building deep and lasting connections requires time and effort, as well as the willingness to navigate the complexities of human interaction. Patience enables us to listen actively, communicate openly, and resolve conflicts with empathy and understanding. By investing in our relationships, we create a network of support that enriches our lives and enhances our development.

Patience also encourages us to embrace the process of self-discovery. Personal growth involves exploring our values, beliefs, and aspirations, and this journey of self-exploration cannot be rushed. It requires patience to sit with our thoughts and emotions, to reflect on our experiences, and to gain insight into who we are and what we truly want. This introspection allows us to align our actions with our authentic selves, fostering a sense of fulfillment and purpose.

In addition, patience plays a vital role in the development of new skills and habits. Whether we are learning a new language, adopting a healthier lifestyle, or cultivating a creative practice, mastery takes time and dedication. Patience allows us to persevere through the initial stages of learning, when progress may be slow and challenging. It instills in us the discipline to practice consistently, knowing that each small step contributes to our overall growth and success.

The practice of patience also extends to our interactions with the broader world. In an age of instant communication and rapid technological advancements, it can be easy to become overwhelmed by the constant influx of information and stimuli. Patience invites us to slow down, to disconnect from the noise, and to cultivate a deeper connection with the present moment. This mindfulness allows us to appreciate the beauty and richness of life, to savor our experiences, and to find joy in the journey.

Furthermore, patience teaches us the importance of resilience and perseverance. Life is filled with challenges and uncertainties, and it is through patience that we develop the strength to endure and overcome them. It empowers us to face difficulties with courage and determination, knowing that growth often occurs in the midst of adversity. By cultivating patience, we build the resilience needed to navigate life's ups and downs, emerging stronger and more capable.

Ultimately, the role of patience in personal growth is multifaceted, touching every aspect of our lives. It is a guiding principle that encourages us to embrace the journey, to value the process, and to trust in our capacity for change. By cultivating patience, we create a foundation for growth that is rooted in self-compassion, resilience, and authenticity. This foundation allows us to evolve into the individuals we aspire to be, enriching our lives and the lives of those around us.

In a world that often prioritizes speed and efficiency, patience provides a counterbalance, reminding us of the beauty and wisdom that comes with time. It invites us to slow down, to appreciate the present, and to cultivate a deeper connection with ourselves and the world around us. Through patience, we discover the profound potential for growth that lies within us, unlocking the door to a more fulfilling and meaningful life.

Chapter 2: Mindfulness in Everyday Activities

Practicing Mindfulness in Daily Routines

Mindfulness, a practice rooted in ancient traditions, has found its way into modern life as a powerful tool for enhancing well-being and clarity. At its essence, mindfulness is the art of being fully present and engaged in the moment, aware of our thoughts, feelings, and surroundings without judgment. Integrating mindfulness into daily routines can transform mundane activities into opportunities for growth and reflection, enriching our experience of life.

The journey to practicing mindfulness begins with the recognition that our minds often operate on autopilot. We rush through our days, our thoughts consumed by past regrets or future anxieties, rarely pausing to savor the present moment. This habitual state of distraction can lead to stress, dissatisfaction, and a sense of disconnection from ourselves and others. Mindfulness offers an antidote to this relentless pace, inviting us to slow down and engage with life in a more intentional and meaningful way.

Incorporating mindfulness into daily routines need not be an overwhelming endeavor. It can be as simple as choosing one routine activity and transforming it into a mindful practice. Consider the act of brushing your teeth. Rather than allowing your mind to wander, focus on the sensations—the bristles on your gums, the taste of the toothpaste, the sound of the water. By anchoring your attention to these sensory experiences, you cultivate a sense of presence and awareness.

Similarly, mindful eating is a practice that can transform a routine meal into a deeply satisfying experience. Begin by appreciating the colors, textures, and aromas of your food. As you eat, chew slowly and savor each bite, paying attention to the flavors and sensations. Notice the way your body responds to the nourishment. This practice not only enhances the enjoyment of your meal but also fosters a deeper connection to your body's needs and signals.

Mindful walking is another way to integrate mindfulness into daily life. Whether you're strolling through a park or walking to work, bring your attention to the rhythm of your steps and the sensations in your body. Feel the ground beneath your feet, the air on your skin, and the movement of your muscles. As thoughts arise, acknowledge them without judgment and gently return your focus to the experience of walking. This practice encourages a sense of groundedness and presence, allowing you to connect with your environment and yourself.

The practice of mindful listening can enrich your interactions with others. When engaged in conversation, give your full attention to the speaker, setting aside distractions and preconceived notions. Listen not only to the words but also to the emotions and intentions behind them. By offering your presence and empathy, you create a space for authentic connection and understanding. This practice can deepen relationships and enhance communication, fostering a sense of mutual respect and trust.

Mindfulness can also be woven into the fabric of your workday. Begin by setting an intention for your day, a guiding principle that aligns with your values and goals. Throughout the day, take moments to pause and check in with yourself. Notice any tension or stress in your body, and take a few deep breaths to release it. As you engage in tasks, focus on one thing at a time, bringing your full attention to the present moment. This approach not only enhances productivity but also promotes a sense of calm and balance.

Incorporating mindfulness into daily routines involves cultivating a mindset of curiosity and openness. Rather than viewing tasks as chores to be completed, approach them with a sense of wonder and exploration. This shift in perspective can transform even the most mundane activities into opportunities for learning and growth. By embracing each moment with mindfulness, you awaken to the richness and beauty of life.

The practice of mindfulness extends beyond individual activities, encompassing the overall rhythm and flow of your day. Create rituals that support mindfulness, such as starting and ending your day with a few moments of quiet reflection or meditation. These rituals serve as anchors, grounding you in the present and providing a sense of continuity and stability amidst the busyness of life.

As you integrate mindfulness into your daily routines, be gentle with yourself. Mindfulness is a practice, and like any skill, it requires time and patience to develop. There will be moments when your mind wanders or you become caught up in the demands of the day. When this happens, simply acknowledge it and gently return your focus to the present moment. This practice of returning, again and again, is at the heart of mindfulness, fostering resilience and self-compassion.

Ultimately, practicing mindfulness in daily routines is a journey of discovery, one that invites you to cultivate a deeper connection with yourself and the world around you. It is an invitation to live with intention and authenticity, to embrace each moment with presence and gratitude. Through mindfulness, you can transform the ordinary into the extraordinary, enriching your life with a sense of peace, purpose, and fulfillment.

The Joy of Simple Pleasures

In a world that often equates happiness with material wealth and grand achievements, the joy of simple pleasures remains a timeless and accessible source of fulfillment. These modest delights, easily overlooked in the pursuit of larger goals, offer profound happiness and a deep sense of contentment. Reconnecting with the simplicity of everyday moments invites us to appreciate the richness of life, grounding us in gratitude and presence.

Consider the gentle warmth of the morning sun on your face as you sip your first cup of coffee. The aroma fills the air, a comforting presence that signals the start of a new day. As you take that initial sip, the rich flavors dance on your palate, awakening your senses and enveloping you in a moment of pure joy. This simple pleasure sets the tone for the day, reminding you to pause and savor the little things that often go unnoticed.

The laughter shared with a friend, the kind that bubbles up from within and leaves you breathless, is another such treasure. This spontaneous joy, rooted in genuine connection and shared experiences, creates a bond that transcends words. It is in these moments that we are reminded of the importance of relationships and the warmth they bring to our lives. These shared laughs, though fleeting, leave a lasting impression on our hearts.

Nature, too, offers an abundance of simple pleasures, freely available to those willing to pause and take notice. The delicate sound of leaves rustling in the wind, the vibrant colors of a sunset painting the sky, or the gentle rhythm of waves lapping against the shore—all these evoke a sense of wonder and peace. Immersing ourselves in nature's beauty allows us to recalibrate, to find solace in the world's natural rhythms, and to appreciate the intricate tapestry of life.

The act of creation, whether through art, music, or writing, is a simple pleasure that taps into our innate desire for expression. When we create, we engage with the world in a way that is uniquely ours, channeling our emotions and thoughts into tangible forms. This process of creation, often more rewarding than the finished product, provides a sense of accomplishment and fulfillment. It connects us to something greater than ourselves, a testament to the beauty of human creativity.

Another simple pleasure lies in the realm of culinary experiences. The act of preparing a meal, the careful selection of ingredients, the alchemy of flavors coming together, can be a meditation in itself. Sharing this meal with loved ones, the clinking of glasses and the exchange of stories around the table, transforms it into a celebration of togetherness. Food, in its simplest form, nourishes not only the body but also the soul, fostering a sense of community and belonging.

The joy of simple pleasures is also found in the practice of gratitude. Taking a moment each day to reflect on the things we are thankful for shifts our focus from what we lack to what we have. This practice, though simple, can have a profound impact on our overall well-being. It encourages us to appreciate the present moment, to recognize the abundance in our lives, and to cultivate a mindset of positivity and contentment.

Reading a book, losing yourself in the pages of a story, provides another avenue for simple joy. The act of reading transports us to different worlds, introduces us to new perspectives, and allows us to experience the lives of others. It is a journey of discovery that can be both enlightening and entertaining. The quiet solitude of reading offers a respite from the noise of everyday life, a chance to recharge and reflect.

The joy found in simple pleasures is intimately tied to the concept of mindfulness. By being fully present and engaged in the moment, we open ourselves to the beauty and wonder of life's small offerings. This mindfulness allows us to experience the world with fresh eyes, to find delight in the ordinary, and to cultivate a deep sense of appreciation for the here and now.

Incorporating simple pleasures into daily life requires a shift in perspective, a conscious decision to prioritize moments of joy amidst the busyness of modern living. It involves letting go of the need for constant achievement and embracing the idea that happiness can be found in the most unexpected places. By doing so, we create a life that is not only rich in experiences but also grounded in contentment.

The power of simple pleasures lies in their accessibility. They are available to anyone, regardless of circumstances, and serve as a reminder that happiness is not reserved for monumental events or milestones. Instead, it is woven into the fabric of everyday life, waiting to be discovered in the small, seemingly insignificant moments that often pass us by.

In a world that often prioritizes the pursuit of wealth and success, the joy of simple pleasures offers a timeless counterbalance. It invites us to slow down, to appreciate the present, and to find fulfillment in the here and now. By embracing these simple joys, we cultivate a life that is both meaningful and abundant, rich in the small moments that bring us true happiness. Through this lens, we come to understand that the essence of a joyful life lies not in the grandiose but in the beautifully ordinary.

Mindful Eating and Savoring Each Bite

Mindful eating transforms an everyday necessity into a profound practice of awareness, transforming meals into moments of mindfulness and deep appreciation. In an age where fast food and hurried meals dominate, the art of savoring each bite has become a lost gem. Embracing mindful eating not only nourishes the body but also cultivates a healthier relationship with food and enhances overall well-being.

The practice of mindful eating begins with the act of slowing down. In our fast-paced world, meals are often consumed in haste, an afterthought amidst the day's activities. By consciously choosing to slow down, we create space to truly engage with the food before us. This involves setting aside distractions, turning off screens, and allowing ourselves to be fully present at the table. It is a commitment to honor the meal as a moment of pause and reflection, rather than a task to be completed.

Mindful eating invites us to engage our senses fully. Before taking the first bite, take a moment to observe the colors and textures of the food, to inhale the aromas that rise from the plate. Each of these sensory experiences contributes to the anticipation and enjoyment of the meal. As you begin to eat, focus on the flavors that unfold on your palate, the interplay of sweet, savory, bitter, and umami. Notice the textures, the crunch or creaminess, and how they change with each chew. This sensory engagement enriches the eating experience, bringing a heightened awareness to each bite.

The act of chewing is central to mindful eating, offering an opportunity to savor and appreciate the food fully. Rather than rushing through the meal, take the time to chew each bite thoroughly, allowing the flavors to develop and unfold. This not only enhances the enjoyment of the meal but also aids digestion, as the process of chewing signals the body to prepare for the absorption of nutrients. By focusing on the rhythmic motion of chewing, we anchor ourselves in the present moment, cultivating a deeper connection to the act of eating.

Mindful eating also involves cultivating an awareness of hunger and satiety cues. In a world where food is often consumed mindlessly, it can be easy to lose touch with the body's natural signals. Before beginning a meal, take a moment to assess your hunger level. Are you eating out of genuine hunger, or is it driven by emotion or habit? As you eat, periodically check in with your body to gauge your level of fullness. This practice encourages a more intuitive approach to eating, allowing us to honor our body's needs and avoid overeating.

Emotional awareness is a critical aspect of mindful eating, inviting us to explore the emotions that often accompany our eating habits. Food can be a source of comfort, a way to cope with stress or difficult emotions. By bringing mindfulness to the table, we can begin to recognize these patterns and develop healthier ways of responding to our emotional landscape. This involves acknowledging emotions without judgment and exploring alternative coping strategies that do not rely solely on food.

Mindful eating is not limited to the act of consuming food; it extends to the entire experience of a meal, from preparation to consumption. Engaging mindfully in the preparation of food can be a meditative practice in itself. The process of selecting ingredients, washing, chopping, and cooking can become a ritual of mindfulness, a way to connect with the nourishment we provide for ourselves and our loved ones. By approaching food preparation with care and intention, we cultivate a deeper appreciation for the meal and the effort involved in bringing it to the table.

The practice of gratitude is an integral component of mindful eating. Taking a moment to express gratitude for the food before us, for the hands that prepared it, and for the earth that provided it, fosters a sense of connection and appreciation. This gratitude extends beyond the meal, encouraging a mindset of abundance and mindfulness in other aspects of life. By acknowledging the interconnectedness of our food system, we develop a greater awareness of the impact our choices have on the environment and communities.

Mindful eating can be a communal experience, enriching relationships and fostering connection. Sharing a meal with others offers an opportunity to practice mindfulness collectively. Engaging in meaningful conversation, listening actively, and being present with those around the table creates a sense of community and belonging. This shared experience of mindfulness can deepen bonds and enhance the enjoyment of the meal, transforming it into a celebration of togetherness.

It's important to acknowledge that mindful eating is a practice, one that requires patience and intention. Like any skill, it develops over time, and there will be moments when distractions and habits intrude. When this happens, gently bring your focus back to the present moment, to the sensory experience of eating. This practice of returning, again and again, is at the heart of mindfulness, fostering resilience and self-compassion.

The benefits of mindful eating extend beyond the table, influencing overall well-being and quality of life. By cultivating a mindful approach to eating, we develop a healthier relationship with food, one that is rooted in awareness and appreciation. This mindfulness fosters a sense of balance and harmony, allowing us to enjoy the pleasures of eating while honoring our body's needs.

Incorporating mindful eating into daily life invites us to rediscover the joy of savoring each bite, to cultivate gratitude for the nourishment we receive, and to create a deeper connection to ourselves and the world around us. It is a practice that enriches not only our meals but also our lives, offering a pathway to greater health, happiness, and fulfillment. Through mindful eating, we come to understand that food is more than sustenance; it is a celebration of life and a reflection of our connection to the earth and each other.

Cultivating Gratitude and Appreciation

Gratitude, a simple yet profound practice, holds the power to transform our lives by shifting our focus from what we lack to the abundance that surrounds us. In the pursuit of happiness and fulfillment, cultivating gratitude and appreciation becomes an essential tool, allowing us to recognize and cherish the richness of our experiences. By embracing gratitude, we open our hearts to joy, deepen our connections with others, and foster a mindset that enhances our overall well-being.

The journey of cultivating gratitude begins with awareness—recognizing the moments in our daily lives for which we are thankful. This practice involves a conscious effort to notice and appreciate the positive aspects of our experiences, no matter how small they may seem. It is a deliberate choice to focus on the good, to savor the present moment, and to acknowledge the gifts that life offers. By doing so, we create a mental shift that encourages positivity and contentment.

One practical way to cultivate gratitude is by keeping a gratitude journal. Each day, set aside a few moments to reflect on the things you are grateful for and write them down. These can range from simple pleasures, like a warm cup of tea, to significant events, like a promotion at work. The act of writing reinforces the appreciation, making it more tangible and memorable. Over time, this practice builds a repository of positive experiences that can be revisited during challenging times, serving as a reminder of the abundance in our lives.

Expressing gratitude to others is another powerful way to cultivate appreciation. Whether through words, gestures, or acts of kindness, acknowledging the contributions of those around us strengthens relationships and fosters a sense of connection. A heartfelt thank you, a thoughtful note, or a small token of appreciation can have a profound impact, not only on the recipient but also on the giver. This exchange of gratitude creates a positive feedback loop, enhancing the sense of community and belonging.

Gratitude extends beyond personal interactions, encompassing our relationship with the world around us. Nature, in its infinite beauty and complexity, offers countless opportunities for appreciation. The vibrant colors of a sunrise, the soothing sound of rain, or the delicate petals of a flower—each provides a moment to pause and marvel at the wonders of the natural world. By immersing ourselves in nature's beauty, we cultivate a sense of awe and reverence, nurturing a deeper connection to the earth and its cycles.

Mindfulness plays a crucial role in the practice of gratitude, encouraging us to be fully present and engaged in our experiences. By slowing down and savoring each moment, we become more attuned to the beauty and blessings that surround us. This mindfulness allows us to notice the subtleties that often go unnoticed in the rush of daily life, fostering a sense of appreciation for the here and now. Through mindful awareness, we cultivate a mindset that is open to joy and receptive to the abundance of life.

Gratitude also involves acknowledging the lessons learned from adversity. Life is filled with challenges, and it is through these experiences that we often gain the most profound insights. By reframing difficulties as opportunities for growth, we can cultivate gratitude for the lessons they impart. This shift in perspective encourages resilience and empowers us to navigate life's ups and downs with grace and equanimity. Embracing gratitude in the face of adversity allows us to find meaning and purpose, even amidst hardship.

Incorporating gratitude into daily routines can have a transformative impact on our overall well-being. Research has shown that gratitude is linked to increased happiness, improved physical health, and stronger relationships. By making gratitude a regular practice, we cultivate a mindset that enhances our quality of life and fosters a deep sense of fulfillment. This practice is not about denying the challenges we face but rather about celebrating the beauty and richness that coexist with them.

The practice of gratitude extends to the realm of self-compassion, inviting us to appreciate and honor ourselves. Often, we are quick to criticize and judge ourselves, focusing on perceived shortcomings rather than acknowledging our strengths and achievements. By cultivating gratitude for the person we are, we nurture a sense of self-worth and acceptance. This self-compassion fosters a healthier relationship with ourselves, allowing us to embrace our imperfections and celebrate our uniqueness.

Gratitude also invites us to embrace the present moment, to let go of the need for more and to find contentment in the now. In a culture that often equates success with accumulation and achievement, gratitude offers a counterbalance, reminding us that true fulfillment lies not in external possessions but in the richness of our experiences and connections. By focusing on the present and appreciating what we have, we create a life that is grounded in contentment and joy.

Cultivating gratitude is an ongoing journey, one that requires intention and practice. It is a mindset that can be nurtured and developed over time, leading to profound shifts in perspective and well-being. As we embrace gratitude, we open ourselves to the abundance and beauty that surrounds us, enriching our lives and the lives of those around us.

The power of gratitude lies not in its complexity but in its simplicity. It is a practice that is accessible to all, regardless of circumstances, and offers a pathway to greater happiness and fulfillment. By choosing gratitude, we transform the way we experience the world, fostering a sense of appreciation that permeates every aspect of our lives. Through gratitude, we discover the joy of living with an open heart, embracing the present with wonder and appreciation.

The Art of Single-Tasking

In a world that glorifies multitasking, the art of single-tasking emerges as a powerful counterbalance, offering a pathway to increased focus, productivity, and satisfaction. While the ability to juggle multiple tasks simultaneously is often celebrated, research suggests that it can lead to decreased efficiency and greater stress. Embracing single-tasking allows us to immerse ourselves fully in one task at a time, fostering a deeper connection to our work and enhancing the quality of our output.

The practice of single-tasking begins with the conscious decision to prioritize one task above all others. This requires setting clear intentions and boundaries, a commitment to dedicating time and energy to a singular pursuit without succumbing to the distractions that vie for our attention. By doing so, we create an environment that supports concentration and encourages a state of flow, where we are fully engaged and absorbed in the task at hand.

Creating a conducive workspace is crucial to the art of single-tasking. This involves minimizing external distractions by organizing your environment to support focus. Clear your desk of unnecessary clutter, silence notifications on your devices, and establish a routine that signals the start of focused work time. By creating a physical space that aligns with your intention to single-task, you set the stage for deeper concentration and creativity.

Time management is another key aspect of single-tasking. Allocating specific blocks of time to dedicated tasks allows us to fully engage without the pressure of competing priorities. The Pomodoro Technique, which involves working in focused intervals followed by short breaks, can be an effective way to maintain concentration and manage mental fatigue. By structuring our time in this way, we harness the benefits of single-tasking while also allowing for necessary periods of rest and rejuvenation.

The art of single-tasking also involves cultivating awareness of our mental and emotional states. Often, we turn to multitasking as a way to avoid discomfort or boredom, seeking stimulation from multiple sources to fill the void. By practicing mindfulness, we become more attuned to these tendencies, allowing us to address the underlying emotions and refocus our attention on the present task. Mindfulness encourages us to embrace the process rather than the outcome, fostering a deeper appreciation for the work itself.

A significant benefit of single-tasking is the opportunity for enhanced creativity and problem-solving. When we dedicate our full attention to a task, we open ourselves to new insights and perspectives that may have been overlooked in a divided state of mind. This focused engagement allows us to explore ideas more deeply, leading to innovative solutions and breakthroughs. By giving ourselves the space to fully immerse in the creative process, we cultivate an environment where inspiration can flourish.

Single-tasking also contributes to greater satisfaction and well-being. By completing tasks with intention and care, we experience a sense of accomplishment and pride in our work. This process of fully engaging with one task at a time fosters a sense of mastery, enhancing our confidence and self-esteem. Moreover, it reduces the stress and overwhelm that often accompany multitasking, allowing us to approach our work with a sense of calm and balance.

The art of single-tasking extends beyond professional endeavors to encompass all areas of life. Whether it is spending quality time with loved ones, engaging in a hobby, or participating in self-care activities, the practice of being fully present enhances the richness of our experiences. By dedicating our attention to the people and activities that matter most, we deepen our connections and cultivate a greater sense of fulfillment.

Developing the habit of single-tasking requires patience and practice, as it challenges the ingrained tendencies to seek stimulation from multiple sources. It involves letting go of the need to constantly check emails, messages, or social media, and embracing the idea that quality trumps quantity. This shift in mindset encourages us to value depth over breadth, creating a life that is grounded in meaningful experiences and authentic connections.

The journey to mastering the art of single-tasking is one of self-discovery and growth. It invites us to examine our priorities, to reflect on what truly matters, and to align our actions with our values. By cultivating the ability to focus on one task at a time, we develop a greater sense of clarity and purpose, empowering us to live with intention and authenticity.

In an era where attention is a valuable commodity, the art of single-tasking offers a pathway to reclaiming our focus and enhancing our well-being. It is a practice that encourages us to slow down, to savor the process, and to engage fully with the world around us. By embracing single-tasking, we create a life that is not only more productive but also more meaningful and fulfilling. Through this practice, we come to understand that true success lies not in the quantity of tasks completed, but in the quality of our engagement and the depth of our experiences.

Mindful Communication and Listening

Mindful communication is an art that transcends mere words, inviting us to engage with others in a way that is genuine, empathetic, and deeply connected. In a world where conversations often occur amidst distractions and divided attention, the practice of mindful communication and listening emerges as a powerful means to foster understanding, build stronger relationships, and create a sense of presence in our interactions.

The foundation of mindful communication lies in the practice of active listening. This involves fully concentrating on what is being said, rather than passively hearing the speaker's words. Active listening requires setting aside distractions, such as phones or other devices, and dedicating our full attention to the person speaking. By doing so, we signal our respect and interest, creating an environment where open and honest communication can flourish.

Active listening also involves being attentive to non-verbal cues, such as body language, facial expressions, and tone of voice. These elements often convey more about the speaker's emotions and intentions than words alone. By tuning in to these signals, we gain a deeper understanding of the speaker's message and can respond with greater empathy and insight. This heightened awareness allows us to connect on a more meaningful level, fostering trust and rapport.

Practicing presence is another crucial aspect of mindful communication. It involves being fully present in the moment, not allowing our minds to wander to past interactions or future tasks. This presence encourages us to engage with the conversation as it unfolds, responding thoughtfully and authentically. When we are present, we bring a sense of calm and focus to the interaction, allowing us to communicate with clarity and intention.

Mindful communication also requires cultivating an attitude of curiosity and openness. This means approaching conversations with a willingness to learn and understand, rather than simply waiting for our turn to speak. By asking open-ended questions and encouraging dialogue, we create a space where diverse perspectives can be explored and valued. This openness fosters a sense of mutual respect and collaboration, enriching the quality of our interactions.

Empathy plays a vital role in mindful communication, inviting us to step into the shoes of the speaker and see the world from their perspective. This empathetic approach allows us to connect with the emotions and experiences of others, creating a sense of shared understanding. By acknowledging and validating the speaker's feelings, we demonstrate compassion and support, strengthening the bond between us.

In addition to listening, mindful communication involves being aware of our own communication style and the impact it has on others. This requires reflecting on the words we choose, the tone we use, and the body language we convey. By communicating with intention and authenticity, we express our thoughts and feelings in a way that is respectful and considerate. This self-awareness enhances our ability to convey our message effectively and fosters a sense of integrity in our interactions.

The practice of mindful communication extends to the way we navigate conflict and disagreement. Rather than approaching these situations with defensiveness or aggression, mindful communication encourages us to listen with an open heart and mind. This involves acknowledging differing viewpoints and seeking common ground, rather than focusing solely on winning the argument. By approaching conflict with empathy and understanding, we create opportunities for resolution and growth.

Mindful communication also invites us to cultivate patience and restraint, particularly in challenging conversations. This involves taking a moment to pause and reflect before responding, allowing us to choose our words carefully and avoid reactive or impulsive responses. By practicing patience, we create space for thoughtful and respectful dialogue, enhancing the quality of our interactions.

Incorporating mindfulness into our communication practices can have a transformative impact on our relationships and overall well-being. By engaging in mindful communication, we create a sense of connection and understanding that enriches our interactions with others. This practice fosters a sense of belonging and community, allowing us to build stronger and more meaningful relationships.

The benefits of mindful communication extend beyond personal interactions to encompass professional and social contexts. In the workplace, mindful communication can enhance collaboration and teamwork, fostering a culture of openness and innovation. In social settings, it encourages inclusivity and respect, creating environments where diverse voices are heard and valued.

Developing the habit of mindful communication requires intention and practice. It involves letting go of the need to dominate conversations or prove our point, and embracing the idea that understanding and connection are more valuable than being right. This shift in mindset encourages us to approach communication with humility and curiosity, creating a life that is grounded in meaningful and authentic interactions.

As we cultivate the art of mindful communication, we embark on a journey of self-discovery and growth. This practice invites us to reflect on our values and priorities, aligning our actions with our desire to connect and understand. By embracing mindful communication, we create a life that is not only more connected but also more fulfilling and harmonious.

In a world where communication is often superficial and fragmented, mindful communication offers a pathway to deeper understanding and connection. It is a practice that encourages us to engage with others in a way that is genuine, empathetic, and present. By embracing mindful communication, we transform the way we interact with the world, fostering relationships that are grounded in trust, respect, and mutual understanding. Through this practice, we come to understand that true communication is not just about exchanging words, but about creating a shared experience of connection and presence.

Chapter 3: Connecting with Nature

The Healing Power of the Natural World

The natural world, in its vastness and beauty, offers a sanctuary for healing and renewal. In an age where technology often dominates our lives, reconnecting with nature can provide profound benefits that nurture both body and soul. The healing power of nature lies in its ability to ground us, to remind us of our connection to the earth, and to offer solace amidst the chaos of modern life.

A walk through a forest, the gentle rustle of leaves underfoot, the dappled sunlight filtering through the canopy—these simple experiences have the power to calm the mind and rejuvenate the spirit. Nature's rhythms, so different from the frenetic pace of human life, invite us to slow down, to breathe deeply, and to be present. The practice of forest bathing, or shinrin-yoku, has gained popularity for its therapeutic effects, promoting tranquility and reducing stress levels. By immersing ourselves in the natural world, we create space for reflection and renewal.

The sensory experiences offered by nature are a balm for the senses. The vibrant hues of a sunset, the soothing sound of ocean waves, the earthy scent of rain on dry soil—each engages our senses in a way that artificial environments cannot replicate. These sensory interactions anchor us in the present moment, drawing us away from the distractions of daily life. The act of observing nature's beauty fosters a sense of wonder and gratitude, enhancing our overall well-being.

Nature also offers a sense of perspective, reminding us of the larger cycles of life. The changing seasons, the ebb and flow of tides, the migration of birds—all underscore the interconnectedness of life on earth. By witnessing these natural cycles, we gain a deeper understanding of our place within the world. This perspective encourages humility and acceptance, allowing us to approach life's challenges with greater resilience and grace.

Physical activity in natural settings further enhances the healing power of the outdoors. Whether hiking through mountains, cycling along a riverbank, or practicing yoga in a park, the combination of movement and nature provides a powerful antidote to stress and fatigue. The physical benefits of outdoor activity are well-documented, including improved cardiovascular health, increased energy levels, and enhanced mood. The natural environment encourages us to engage our bodies in a way that is both invigorating and restorative.

The healing power of the natural world is not limited to individual experiences; it also fosters a sense of community and connection. Shared experiences in nature, such as group hikes or community gardening, create opportunities for bonding and collaboration. These communal activities promote social well-being, reducing feelings of isolation and fostering a sense of belonging. The shared appreciation for nature's beauty and bounty strengthens relationships and builds a sense of community.

Nature's healing power extends to its ability to inspire creativity and innovation. The tranquility and beauty of natural settings create an environment conducive to creative thinking and problem-solving. Many artists, writers, and thinkers have drawn inspiration from nature's landscapes, finding solace and inspiration in its forms and colors. By engaging with nature, we open ourselves to new ideas and perspectives, fostering creativity and innovation.

The benefits of nature are not confined to pristine wilderness; even small urban green spaces can provide refuge and renewal. Parks, gardens, and green rooftops offer urban dwellers access to nature's healing power, providing a counterbalance to the concrete and noise of city life. These green spaces serve as vital oases, offering residents a place to relax, reflect, and reconnect with the natural world.

Cultivating a relationship with nature requires intention and mindfulness. It involves setting aside time to engage with the outdoors, whether through daily walks, weekend excursions, or seasonal adventures. By prioritizing time in nature, we honor the importance of our connection to the earth and its role in our well-being. This commitment fosters a deeper appreciation for the natural world and encourages us to be stewards of its beauty and resources.

Incorporating nature into our daily lives can have a lasting impact on our mental and physical health. Studies have shown that exposure to natural environments reduces symptoms of anxiety and depression, lowers blood pressure, and boosts immune function. By making nature a regular part of our routine, we enhance our resilience and promote long-term health and happiness.

The healing power of nature invites us to embrace simplicity and presence. It encourages us to step away from the screens and schedules that often dominate our lives and to immerse ourselves in the beauty and tranquility of the natural world. By engaging with nature, we cultivate a sense of balance and harmony, enriching our lives and fostering a deeper connection to the earth and each other.

Ultimately, the healing power of the natural world lies in its ability to remind us of our interconnectedness and interdependence. It is a source of wisdom and comfort, offering lessons in patience, resilience, and renewal. By embracing nature's gifts, we open our hearts to a deeper understanding of ourselves and our place within the world. Through this connection, we find healing, inspiration, and a profound sense of belonging.

Slowing Down Through Outdoor Activities

The frenetic pace of modern life often leaves us yearning for moments of stillness, where time stretches and the world quiets. Engaging in outdoor activities offers a gateway to slowing down, providing a space where we can reconnect with ourselves and the natural world. These activities invite us to step away from the digital noise and immerse ourselves in the present moment, fostering a sense of peace and clarity.

Venturing into nature provides a unique opportunity to experience the world at a different tempo. Hiking, for instance, encourages us to match our pace to the rhythm of the earth, each step a deliberate movement forward. The trail unfolds at its own speed, revealing vistas and landscapes that remind us of the beauty in patience. As we navigate paths, we connect with the nuances of the environment—the crunch of leaves, the scent of pine, the distant call of a bird. These sensory experiences ground us, drawing our focus away from the past or future and into the now.

Cycling through scenic routes offers a similar respite, where the wind against our skin and the steady cadence of pedaling create a meditative rhythm. Each turn of the wheel propels us further from the rush of everyday concerns, allowing us to explore new terrains both externally and internally. The journey becomes a space for reflection, where thoughts can wander freely and solutions to problems often arise organically. As we cover miles, the simplicity of the motion fosters a sense of liberation and mindfulness.

Water-based activities, such as kayaking or paddleboarding, present another avenue for deceleration. The gentle lapping of water against the hull and the rhythmic dip of the paddle invite a state of flow, where time seems to dissolve. The vastness of open water encourages introspection and a sense of wonder, as we become attuned to the natural rhythms of tides and currents. These activities cultivate a profound connection to the aquatic world, reminding us of the tranquility that lies in surrendering to the moment.

Gardening, though often overlooked as an outdoor activity, offers a deeply satisfying way to slow down and engage with nature. The tactile experience of planting seeds, tending to soil, and nurturing growth creates a direct connection to the earth. The gradual transformation from seedling to bloom mirrors our own journey, teaching us patience and the rewards of consistent care. As we watch our gardens flourish, we experience the satisfaction of nurturing life and the simple joy of witnessing nature's cycles.

Mindful walking, or walking meditation, is another practice that emphasizes the art of slowing down. This activity involves walking with intention and awareness, focusing on the sensation of each step and the environment around us. The pace is unhurried, inviting a deep sense of presence and calm. As we walk, we cultivate mindfulness, allowing thoughts to arise and pass without judgment. This practice encourages us to let go of the need to hurry and to embrace the journey itself.

Engaging in these outdoor activities not only slows our pace but also provides a host of physical and mental benefits. Physical activity in nature enhances cardiovascular health, boosts mood, and reduces stress levels. The immersive experience of being outdoors stimulates the senses and nurtures creativity, providing a fertile ground for inspiration and new ideas. The natural environment acts as a buffer against the pressures of modern life, offering a sanctuary for recovery and reflection.

Slowing down through outdoor activities also fosters a deeper connection to the surrounding world. As we immerse ourselves in natural settings, we become more attuned to the intricate web of life that sustains us. This awareness encourages a sense of stewardship and responsibility, motivating us to protect and preserve the environments we cherish. Our connection to the earth deepens, enriching our lives with a sense of purpose and belonging.

The practice of slowing down through outdoor activities is accessible to all, regardless of location or lifestyle. Urban parks, community gardens, and nearby trails offer opportunities for engagement with nature, even amidst the hustle of city life. By prioritizing time outdoors, we create a rhythm that balances the demands of daily life with moments of tranquility and presence.

Incorporating outdoor activities into our routine requires intention and commitment. It involves setting aside time to engage with nature, whether through daily walks, weekend excursions, or seasonal adventures. This commitment honors the importance of our connection to the earth and its role in our well-being. By nurturing this relationship, we cultivate a life that is grounded in balance and harmony.

Ultimately, the practice of slowing down through outdoor activities invites us to embrace the richness of the present moment. It encourages us to let go of the need for constant movement and to savor the beauty of stillness. By engaging with nature, we create a space for renewal and reflection, enriching our lives with experiences that nourish both body and soul. Through this practice, we find solace and strength, discovering that the art of slowing down is not a retreat from life but a deeper engagement with it.

The Practice of Forest Bathing

Forest bathing, known as shinrin-yoku in Japan, invites us to immerse our senses in the tranquility of the forest, offering a refuge from the demands of modern life. This practice transcends a mere walk in the woods; it is an intentional experience that engages all the senses, fostering a deep connection with nature and promoting holistic well-being. Rooted in the understanding that nature has a profound impact on our health, forest bathing encourages us to slow down and savor the beauty and serenity of the natural world.

The origins of forest bathing can be traced to Japan, where it was developed in the 1980s as a response to the increasing urbanization and technological overload experienced by society. The Japanese Ministry of Agriculture, Forestry, and Fisheries coined the term shinrin-yoku, recognizing the therapeutic effects of spending time in forests. Since then, the practice has gained recognition worldwide for its ability to reduce stress, enhance mood, and boost physical health.

Engaging in forest bathing begins with setting an intention to connect with the natural environment. This requires leaving behind the distractions of daily life, such as electronic devices and mental clutter, and approaching the forest with an open heart and mind. It involves slowing our pace and allowing ourselves to be fully present, observing the sights, sounds, and sensations that surround us. By doing so, we create a space for reflection and renewal, inviting a sense of peace and clarity.

The sensory immersion of forest bathing is at the heart of its healing power. The gentle rustle of leaves, the earthy scent of moss, the play of light through the canopy—all these elements engage our senses in a way that is both calming and invigorating. This multisensory experience anchors us in the present moment, drawing our attention away from worries and distractions. As we attune ourselves to the natural world, we cultivate a sense of wonder and gratitude, enhancing our overall well-being.

Scientific research supports the benefits of forest bathing, highlighting its positive impact on both mental and physical health. Studies have shown that spending time in forests can lower cortisol levels, the hormone associated with stress, and reduce symptoms of anxiety and depression. The practice also enhances immune function, with exposure to phytoncides—natural compounds released by trees—boosting the activity of natural killer cells, which play a role in fighting infections and diseases. The calming effects of nature also contribute to lower blood pressure and improved cardiovascular health.

Forest bathing encourages mindfulness, inviting us to engage with the environment in a way that is intentional and reflective. This mindfulness fosters a deeper awareness of our thoughts and emotions, allowing us to observe them without judgment. By cultivating this awareness, we learn to let go of the need to control or fix, embracing the ebb and flow of our inner experiences. This practice of non-judgmental awareness enhances our resilience, equipping us to navigate life's challenges with greater ease and equanimity.

The practice of forest bathing is accessible to all, requiring no special equipment or expertise. It can be practiced in any natural setting, whether a dense forest, a local park, or a small wooded area. The key is to approach the experience with intention and openness, allowing the natural world to guide our exploration. As we wander through the forest, we are encouraged to follow our curiosity, pausing to observe a delicate fern, listen to the call of a distant bird, or feel the texture of bark beneath our fingertips.

A typical forest bathing session may last anywhere from 20 minutes to several hours, depending on individual preferences and the environment. The experience is unstructured, allowing participants to move at their own pace and follow their intuition. Some may choose to sit quietly, observing the interplay of light and shadow, while others may engage in walking meditation, focusing on the sensation of each step. The absence of a fixed agenda encourages a sense of freedom and exploration, inviting us to reconnect with our innate sense of wonder.

The benefits of forest bathing extend beyond the individual, fostering a sense of connection to the larger web of life. As we engage with nature, we become more attuned to the intricate relationships that sustain ecosystems, deepening our appreciation for the interdependence of all living things. This awareness encourages a sense of stewardship and responsibility, motivating us to protect and preserve the environments we cherish.

Incorporating forest bathing into our routine can have a lasting impact on our mental and physical health. By making time for nature, we create a rhythm that balances the demands of daily life with moments of tranquility and presence. This commitment honors the importance of our connection to the earth and its role in our well-being. By nurturing this relationship, we cultivate a life that is grounded in balance and harmony.

Forest bathing is more than a retreat from the world; it is an invitation to engage with it more deeply. It encourages us to embrace the richness of the present moment, to let go of the need for constant movement, and to savor the beauty of stillness. Through this practice, we find solace and strength, discovering that the art of slowing down is not a retreat from life but a deeper engagement with it. The healing power of the forest lies in its ability to remind us of our interconnectedness and interdependence, offering a source of wisdom and comfort that enriches our lives with experiences that nourish both body and soul.

Observing Seasonal Changes

The passage of time is woven seamlessly into the fabric of the natural world, a silent yet powerful reminder of life's cyclical nature. Observing seasonal changes presents an opportunity to connect deeply with these rhythms, offering a sense of continuity and renewal. Each season carries its own unique beauty and lessons, inviting us to engage with the world in a way that is both intentional and reflective.

Spring heralds a time of awakening and rebirth. As the earth begins to warm, dormant seeds stir to life, and a tapestry of color unfurls across the landscape. The air is filled with the scent of blossoms and the sound of birdsong, a symphony of renewal and hope. This season encourages us to embrace new beginnings, to plant the seeds of our own aspirations. It is a time for setting intentions, for cultivating growth both within and around us.

Summer arrives in a blaze of energy and vitality. The sun hangs high, casting long days that invite exploration and adventure. Nature is at its peak, a riot of color and abundance. The warmth of the season encourages us to connect with the outdoors, to immerse ourselves in the bounty of the earth. Whether through gardening, hiking, or simply basking in the sun, summer invites us to celebrate life in all its vibrant forms.

Autumn ushers in a period of transformation and reflection. As the days shorten and temperatures cool, nature begins its preparation for rest. Leaves blush in shades of amber and gold, a stunning display of change and impermanence. This season invites introspection, a time to harvest the fruits of our labor and to let go of what no longer serves us. It is a period of gratitude and reflection, of savoring the richness of experience.

Winter descends with a quiet grace, blanketing the world in stillness and calm. The landscape is stripped bare, revealing the stark beauty of simplicity. This is a time for rest and renewal, for turning inward and seeking warmth. Winter encourages us to slow down, to embrace the comfort of home and hearth. It is an invitation to reflect on the year past and to dream of the year to come.

Observing seasonal changes requires mindfulness and presence. It involves taking the time to notice the subtle shifts in the environment—the first buds of spring, the lengthening shadows of autumn, the crystalline frost of winter. By attuning ourselves to these cycles, we deepen our connection to the natural world and to the cycles within ourselves. This awareness fosters a sense of harmony and balance, reminding us of the interdependence of all life.

Engaging with the seasons can be both a personal and communal practice. Individually, we may choose to journal our observations, capturing the sights, sounds, and emotions each season evokes. This practice encourages reflection and deepens our understanding of the natural rhythms that influence our lives. On a communal level, participating in seasonal traditions and celebrations fosters a sense of belonging and connection. Whether it's gathering for a spring festival or sharing a winter meal, these rituals honor the cycles of nature and strengthen community bonds.

Seasonal changes also offer opportunities for growth and learning. Each season presents unique challenges and gifts, encouraging us to adapt and evolve. By observing how nature responds to these changes, we gain insight into our own capacity for resilience and transformation. This understanding empowers us to navigate life's transitions with grace and confidence, knowing that change is a natural and necessary part of life.

Incorporating the practice of observing seasonal changes into our lives enhances our well-being on multiple levels. Physically, engaging with nature through seasonal activities promotes health and vitality. Mentally, the practice of presence and mindfulness reduces stress and cultivates clarity. Emotionally, the connection to natural rhythms fosters a sense of peace and fulfillment. By aligning ourselves with the cycles of the earth, we create a life that is in harmony with the world around us.

The practice of observing seasonal changes is accessible to all, regardless of location or lifestyle. Whether living in a bustling city or a rural village, opportunities to engage with the seasons abound. Urban parks, community gardens, and nature reserves offer spaces to witness the unfolding of nature's cycles. By prioritizing time in nature, we honor the importance of our connection to the earth and its role in our well-being.

Ultimately, observing seasonal changes invites us to embrace the richness of the present moment. It encourages us to celebrate the beauty of each season, to savor the unique gifts it brings, and to reflect on the lessons it offers. Through this practice, we find solace and strength, discovering that the art of observing nature is not a retreat from life but a deeper engagement with it. The changing seasons remind us of our interconnectedness and interdependence, offering a source of wisdom and comfort that enriches our lives with experiences that nourish both body and soul.

Sustainable Living and Environmental Awareness

Embracing a sustainable lifestyle and cultivating environmental awareness is not merely a trend but an essential shift for preserving our planet's future. In recent decades, the growing impact of human activity on the environment has become increasingly evident. From climate change to biodiversity loss, the challenges are daunting. Yet, each of us holds the power to make a difference by integrating sustainable practices into our daily lives and fostering a deeper connection to the environment.

Sustainable living begins with understanding the intricate relationship between our actions and the planet's well-being. It involves recognizing that the resources we consume—water, energy, food—are finite and that their consumption carries consequences. By becoming more conscious of this interdependence, we can make informed choices that reduce our ecological footprint and contribute to a healthier planet.

One of the most effective ways to embrace sustainability is through mindful consumption. This entails being deliberate about what we buy, choosing products that are ethically sourced, produced with minimal environmental impact, and designed for longevity. Supporting companies that prioritize eco-friendly practices and transparency can drive positive change within industries. Additionally, opting for second-hand or upcycled goods reduces the demand for new resources and minimizes waste.

Reducing waste is a cornerstone of sustainable living. The mantra "reduce, reuse, recycle" provides a framework for minimizing our impact on the environment. Reducing begins with conscious purchasing, choosing items with minimal packaging and avoiding single-use plastics. Reusing encourages creativity and resourcefulness, finding new uses for items rather than discarding them. Recycling ensures that materials are reprocessed and reintroduced into the production cycle, reducing the need for virgin resources.

Energy conservation is another critical aspect of sustainable living. Simple actions, such as turning off lights when leaving a room, unplugging electronics when not in use, and utilizing energy-efficient appliances, can significantly reduce energy consumption. For those with the means, investing in renewable energy sources, such as solar panels or wind turbines, can further decrease reliance on fossil fuels and lower carbon emissions.

Transportation choices also play a significant role in environmental impact. Opting for public transportation, carpooling, biking, or walking reduces greenhouse gas emissions and alleviates traffic congestion. For those who drive, choosing fuel-efficient or electric vehicles can contribute to a reduction in air pollution. Additionally, considering the environmental impact of travel and seeking sustainable tourism options can further align our lifestyle with eco-conscious values.

Sustainable living extends to our food choices, as agriculture is a major contributor to environmental degradation. Embracing a plant-based diet, even partially, can reduce the demand for resource-intensive animal products and lower carbon emissions. Supporting local and organic farmers not only ensures fresher produce but also reduces the energy needed for transportation and the use of harmful pesticides. Composting food scraps transforms waste into nutrient-rich soil, closing the loop in the food cycle and enriching gardens.

Water conservation is equally crucial in sustainable living. Limiting water usage by taking shorter showers, fixing leaks, and using water-efficient fixtures helps preserve this vital resource. Collecting rainwater for garden use and choosing drought-resistant plants can further reduce dependence on municipal water supplies. Understanding the water footprint of products and processes encourages more informed choices.

Beyond individual actions, fostering environmental awareness involves engaging with communities and advocating for policies that support sustainability. Participating in local environmental initiatives, such as tree planting, clean-up events, and educational workshops, builds a sense of connection and collective responsibility. Joining or supporting organizations dedicated to environmental protection amplifies our impact and contributes to systemic change.

Education is a powerful tool for raising environmental awareness. By staying informed about ecological issues and sharing knowledge with others, we contribute to a culture of sustainability. Encouraging curiosity and critical thinking about environmental topics inspires others to adopt eco-friendly practices and advocate for positive change. Schools, workplaces, and community groups can serve as platforms for spreading awareness and fostering a shared commitment to sustainability.

Cultivating a sustainable mindset involves reflecting on our values and priorities. It requires a willingness to question habits and make changes that align with a vision of a healthier planet. This mindset encourages us to consider the long-term impact of our actions and to prioritize the well-being of future generations. By embracing sustainability as a core value, we create a lifestyle that is both fulfilling and responsible.

The journey toward sustainable living is ongoing, marked by continual learning and adaptation. It is a path that requires patience and perseverance, but the rewards are profound. By aligning our actions with the principles of sustainability, we contribute to a world that is more equitable, resilient, and vibrant. This journey invites us to rediscover our connection to the earth, to appreciate the beauty of nature, and to celebrate the abundance that a sustainable lifestyle offers.

In embracing sustainable living and fostering environmental awareness, we become stewards of the planet, committed to nurturing its vitality and diversity. This commitment is not only an obligation but a source of inspiration and hope. As we navigate the challenges of our time, the choices we make today shape the legacy we leave for future generations. Through mindful living and environmental stewardship, we create a world where both people and nature can thrive

Chapter 4: Nurturing Relationships

Building Deeper Connections

In an era where digital communication often eclipses face-to-face interactions, the art of building deeper connections becomes more vital than ever. Human connection lies at the heart of our existence, influencing our well-being, happiness, and sense of belonging. Cultivating meaningful relationships requires intentionality, empathy, and the willingness to engage authentically with others. By nurturing these connections, we enrich our lives and foster a community where individuals feel valued and understood.

Understanding the importance of active listening is foundational to building deeper connections. Listening extends beyond merely hearing words; it involves being fully present and attentive, seeking to understand the speaker's perspective without interruption or judgment. Active listening helps create a safe space where people feel heard and respected. In these moments, we open ourselves to the possibility of genuine connection, fostering trust and mutual understanding.

Empathy plays a pivotal role in forming deeper bonds. By putting ourselves in others' shoes, we gain insight into their experiences, emotions, and motivations. This empathetic approach allows us to respond with compassion and support, strengthening our relationships. Practicing empathy requires vulnerability, as it involves acknowledging and sharing in another's struggles and joys. This vulnerability is a cornerstone of authentic connection, allowing us to relate to others on a profound level.

Effective communication is essential for nurturing meaningful relationships. Clear and open communication fosters transparency and honesty, reducing misunderstandings and conflicts. It involves expressing thoughts and feelings constructively while remaining receptive to feedback. By prioritizing communication, we create an environment where individuals feel comfortable sharing their perspectives and emotions, paving the way for deeper connections.

The practice of gratitude can enhance the quality of our relationships. Expressing appreciation for others' contributions and qualities reinforces positive interactions and strengthens bonds. Acts of gratitude, whether verbal acknowledgments or thoughtful gestures, convey respect and recognition. This practice not only uplifts those around us but also fosters a mindset of appreciation and mindfulness, enriching our connections with others.

Shared experiences serve as a powerful catalyst for building deeper connections. Engaging in activities together, whether hiking, cooking, or volunteering, creates lasting memories and strengthens emotional bonds. These shared moments provide opportunities for collaboration, communication, and laughter, deepening our understanding and appreciation of one another. By prioritizing shared experiences, we cultivate a sense of unity and belonging within our relationships.

Vulnerability, often perceived as a weakness, is a crucial element of authentic connection. Being open about our fears, hopes, and imperfections invites others to do the same, creating a foundation of trust and acceptance. Embracing vulnerability fosters intimacy and allows us to connect on a human level, transcending superficial interactions. By sharing our true selves, we invite deeper connections that are built on mutual respect and understanding.

Setting boundaries is essential for maintaining healthy relationships and fostering deeper connections. Boundaries define our personal limits and protect our emotional well-being. By clearly communicating our boundaries, we establish expectations and create a sense of safety within our relationships. This practice encourages mutual respect and understanding, allowing relationships to flourish while preserving individual autonomy.

Building deeper connections also involves balancing the give-and-take within relationships. Reciprocity ensures that relationships remain equitable and fulfilling, with both parties contributing to and benefiting from the connection. This balance fosters a sense of partnership and shared responsibility, reinforcing the strength and resilience of the relationship. By nurturing reciprocity, we create relationships that are mutually supportive and enriching.

Mindfulness, the practice of being present and fully engaged in the moment, enhances our ability to connect with others. By practicing mindfulness, we become more attuned to our own emotions and those of others, fostering empathy and understanding. Mindfulness encourages us to approach interactions with openness and curiosity, allowing us to connect more deeply and authentically. This practice cultivates a sense of presence and attentiveness, enriching our relationships.

In the digital age, building deeper connections requires navigating the challenges of technology-driven communication.

While digital platforms offer convenience and connectivity, they can also create barriers to genuine interaction. Balancing screen time with face-to-face interactions is crucial for nurturing meaningful relationships. Prioritizing in-person connections allows for richer communication, where non-verbal cues and emotional nuances are fully experienced.

Fostering deeper connections within communities involves engagement and participation. Becoming involved in community events, groups, or initiatives creates opportunities to connect with others who share similar values and interests. These communal interactions foster a sense of belonging and collective purpose, enriching our individual and shared experiences. By actively participating in our communities, we contribute to a culture of connection and support.

Reflecting on personal values and priorities can guide us in building deeper connections. Understanding what matters most to us allows us to align our relationships with our core beliefs and goals. This alignment fosters authenticity and fulfillment, ensuring that our connections are meaningful and supportive. By living in accordance with our values, we attract and nurture relationships that resonate with our true selves.

Ultimately, building deeper connections enriches our lives and enhances our well-being. These connections provide a source of support, inspiration, and joy, contributing to a sense of purpose and fulfillment. As we cultivate meaningful relationships, we create a network of support and understanding that sustains us through life's challenges and celebrations. The art of building deeper connections is a lifelong journey, marked by moments of vulnerability, empathy, and shared experiences. Through this journey, we discover the beauty and power of human connection, creating a world where individuals feel seen, heard, and valued.

The Importance of Presence in Relationships

Presence in relationships transcends the simple act of being physically present with someone; it embodies a deeper commitment to engaging with others on a profound level. In a world filled with constant distractions and demands on our attention, cultivating presence is both a challenge and a necessity. It involves dedicating our full attention to the people we care about, valuing their thoughts, emotions, and experiences as we strive to understand and support them. This practice enriches our relationships, nurtures trust and intimacy, and fosters a sense of belonging and connection.

Being present in a relationship begins with the practice of mindfulness. Mindfulness encourages us to be fully engaged in the moment, to let go of distractions, and to focus on the here and now. This approach allows us to connect with others with clarity and intention, free from the noise of our thoughts and external pressures. By practicing mindfulness, we become more attuned to the needs and emotions of those around us, creating a space where genuine connection can flourish.

Active listening is a cornerstone of presence in relationships. It requires us to listen not only with our ears but with our entire being—our eyes, body language, and emotions. By giving our undivided attention to another person, we demonstrate respect and empathy, validating their experiences and emotions. This level of engagement fosters a sense of safety and trust, encouraging open and honest communication. Active listening involves withholding judgment and resisting the urge to interject with our own thoughts or solutions, allowing the speaker to express themselves fully.

Non-verbal communication plays a significant role in being present. Our body language, facial expressions, and eye contact convey a wealth of information beyond words. By maintaining open and receptive body language, we signal our willingness to engage and connect. Simple gestures, such as nodding in agreement or offering a reassuring smile, reinforce our attentiveness and empathy. Being aware of our non-verbal cues allows us to communicate presence and understanding, deepening our connection with others.

The practice of presence extends to being emotionally available and responsive. This involves recognizing and validating the emotions of others, offering support and understanding without judgment. By being emotionally present, we create a safe space for vulnerability, allowing others to share their innermost thoughts and feelings. This emotional availability fosters intimacy and trust, strengthening the bonds that hold relationships together. It requires us to be attuned to our own emotions, as well, so that we can respond with authenticity and empathy.

Technology, while offering avenues for connection, often poses a challenge to being present. The constant influx of notifications, messages, and digital interactions can pull our attention away from the people physically with us. To cultivate presence, it is essential to set boundaries with technology, prioritizing face-to-face interactions and minimizing distractions. This may involve designating tech-free times or spaces, allowing us to focus fully on the people we are with. By consciously managing our use of technology, we demonstrate our commitment to being present and engaged in our relationships.

Presence in relationships also involves being aware of the dynamics and needs of the relationship itself. Each relationship is unique, shaped by the individuals involved and their shared experiences. By being present, we can recognize and respond to the evolving needs of the relationship, nurturing its growth and development. This may involve adapting our communication styles, addressing conflicts constructively, and celebrating shared milestones. Being attuned to the relationship's needs fosters resilience and adaptability, ensuring its longevity and health.

The importance of presence extends to self-awareness and self-care. To be fully present with others, we must first be present with ourselves, understanding our own needs, boundaries, and emotions. Self-awareness allows us to engage authentically, free from the distractions of unresolved issues or unmet needs. Practicing self-care ensures that we have the emotional and mental resources to be present and supportive in our relationships. By prioritizing our well-being, we enhance our capacity to connect with others meaningfully.

Presence in relationships is not a static state but an ongoing practice. It requires continuous effort and intention, adapting to the changing circumstances and needs of those we care about. This practice invites us to remain curious and open, to approach each interaction with a willingness to learn and grow. By committing to presence, we cultivate relationships that are dynamic, resilient, and deeply fulfilling.

The rewards of being present in relationships are profound. Presence fosters a sense of belonging and connection, creating a network of support and understanding that sustains us through life's challenges and joys. It enriches our lives with meaningful interactions and shared experiences, contributing to a sense of purpose and fulfillment. Being present allows us to celebrate the beauty of human connection, to experience the richness of life in all its complexity and depth.

In conclusion, the importance of presence in relationships cannot be overstated. It is a practice that enriches our interactions, nurtures trust and intimacy, and fosters a sense of belonging and connection. By cultivating presence, we create relationships that are meaningful, supportive, and fulfilling, enhancing our lives and the lives of those we care about. This practice invites us to engage with others authentically and empathetically, creating a world where individuals feel seen, heard, and valued. Through the art of presence, we discover the transformative power of human connection, celebrating the beauty and complexity of relationships in all their forms.

Creating Meaningful Interactions

The essence of meaningful interactions lies in their ability to transform ordinary exchanges into moments of genuine connection. In a world dominated by fleeting conversations and digital communication, the art of creating interactions that resonate deeply has become more important than ever. Meaningful interactions are those that leave a lasting impact, fostering understanding, empathy, and a sense of belonging.

They enrich our lives and contribute to the fabric of our relationships, whether personal or professional.

At the heart of meaningful interactions is the practice of active presence. Being truly present means dedicating our full attention to the person we are engaging with, free from distractions and preoccupations. This presence communicates respect and appreciation, signaling that the person deserves our undivided focus. By being present, we create a space where authentic dialogue can flourish, laying the groundwork for a more profound connection.

Empathy is a cornerstone of meaningful interactions, allowing us to connect with others on an emotional level. By striving to understand another's perspective, we open ourselves to shared experiences and emotions. Empathy involves listening with an open heart, acknowledging the feelings and struggles of others without judgment. This empathetic engagement creates a safe space for vulnerability, where individuals feel valued and understood.

Listening, an often underestimated skill, plays a crucial role in crafting meaningful interactions. Active listening requires us to engage fully with what the other person is saying, both verbally and non-verbally. It involves reflecting on their words, asking clarifying questions, and responding thoughtfully. By demonstrating our genuine interest and understanding, we foster an environment where meaningful exchanges can thrive.

Cultivating curiosity enhances the quality of our interactions. Approaching conversations with an open mind and a willingness to learn invites deeper engagement. By asking thoughtful questions and seeking to understand the nuances of another's experiences, we demonstrate our interest and investment in the interaction. This curiosity paves the way for richer exchanges, encouraging others to share more openly and authentically.

Storytelling is a powerful tool for creating meaningful interactions. Sharing personal stories allows us to convey our values, experiences, and emotions in a relatable and engaging manner. It fosters connection by highlighting commonalities and inviting others to share their own narratives. Through storytelling, we create a tapestry of shared experiences, weaving together the threads of our lives in a way that resonates deeply.

Embracing vulnerability is essential for meaningful interactions. By being open about our own experiences, fears, and hopes, we invite others to do the same. This mutual vulnerability fosters trust and intimacy, creating a space where genuine connection can flourish. It requires courage to share our true selves, but the reward is a deeper, more authentic interaction that transcends superficial exchanges.

In the digital age, meaningful interactions can be challenged by the prevalence of technology. While digital platforms offer convenience and connectivity, they often lack the depth and richness of face-to-face interactions. To cultivate meaningful exchanges, it is important to balance digital communication with in-person interactions. Prioritizing face-to-face conversations allows us to engage fully, capturing the nuances of body language, tone, and emotion that enrich our interactions.

Creating meaningful interactions in professional settings involves fostering a culture of openness and collaboration. Encouraging dialogue, valuing diverse perspectives, and promoting mutual respect contribute to a positive and inclusive environment. By prioritizing meaningful exchanges, organizations can enhance teamwork, innovation, and morale, creating a workplace where individuals feel valued and engaged.

The practice of gratitude can enhance the quality of our interactions. Expressing appreciation for the contributions and qualities of others reinforces positive exchanges and strengthens bonds. Acts of gratitude, whether verbal acknowledgments or thoughtful gestures, convey respect and recognition. This practice not only uplifts those around us but also fosters a mindset of appreciation and mindfulness, enriching our connections with others.

Reflecting on personal values and priorities can guide us in creating meaningful interactions. Understanding what matters most to us allows us to align our interactions with our core beliefs and goals. This alignment fosters authenticity and fulfillment, ensuring that our exchanges are meaningful and supportive. By living in accordance with our values, we attract and nurture interactions that resonate with our true selves.

Mindfulness, the practice of being present and fully engaged in the moment, enhances our ability to connect with others. By practicing mindfulness, we become more attuned to our own emotions and those of others, fostering empathy and understanding. Mindfulness encourages us to approach interactions with openness and curiosity, allowing us to connect more deeply and authentically. This practice cultivates a sense of presence and attentiveness, enriching our relationships.

Incorporating humor and playfulness into interactions can create a sense of joy and camaraderie. Laughter and lightheartedness foster a positive atmosphere, breaking down barriers and encouraging openness. By embracing humor, we create an environment where individuals feel comfortable and connected, enhancing the quality of our exchanges.

Ultimately, the art of creating meaningful interactions enriches our lives and enhances our well-being. These interactions provide a source of support, inspiration, and joy, contributing to a sense of purpose and fulfillment. As we cultivate meaningful exchanges, we create a network of support and understanding that sustains us through life's challenges and celebrations. The journey of creating meaningful interactions is ongoing, marked by moments of vulnerability, empathy, and shared experiences. Through this journey, we discover the beauty and power of human connection, creating a world where individuals feel seen, heard, and valued.

Slowing Down Family Life

In the hustle and bustle of modern life, families often find themselves swept up in a whirlwind of activities, obligations, and distractions. The relentless pace can leave little room for meaningful connection, reflection, or simply enjoying each other's company. Yet, there is a profound value in slowing down family life, creating a sanctuary where relationships can flourish, and memories can be made. Embracing a slower pace allows families to reconnect, prioritize what truly matters, and foster an environment of warmth and togetherness.

Slowing down begins with a conscious decision to prioritize quality over quantity. It involves reassessing commitments and making intentional choices about how time is spent. This might mean saying no to certain activities, creating boundaries around work or digital engagement, and carving out time for family rituals. By simplifying schedules and reducing the noise of external demands, families can create space for connection, creativity, and relaxation.

One of the most effective ways to slow down family life is by establishing regular family traditions. Whether it's a weekly game night, a monthly hike, or a Sunday morning pancake breakfast, these rituals provide a sense of rhythm and continuity. They offer opportunities for shared experiences and strengthen familial bonds. Traditions serve as anchors in the ever-changing currents of daily life, creating memories that will be cherished for years to come.

Incorporating mindfulness into family routines fosters a sense of presence and appreciation for the present moment. Mindfulness practices, such as deep breathing, meditation, or simply taking a moment of silence, encourage family members to pause and reflect. By cultivating mindfulness, families can enhance their ability to communicate openly, empathize with one another, and savor the joys of everyday life. This practice nurtures a sense of calm and focus, allowing families to navigate challenges with greater resilience.

Creating designated family time, free from distractions and obligations, is essential for slowing down. This time can be spent engaging in activities that promote connection and interaction, such as cooking a meal together, playing a board game, or going for a walk. These moments provide a break from the demands of the outside world, allowing family members to be fully present with one another. By prioritizing family time, families build a foundation of trust and closeness.

The art of storytelling can play a significant role in slowing down family life. Sharing stories, whether from personal experiences or family history, creates a rich tapestry of connection and understanding. Stories offer insights into values, traditions, and the unique dynamics of a family. They invite conversation and reflection, allowing family members to learn from one another and strengthen their bonds. By embracing storytelling, families create a legacy of shared wisdom and memories.

Slowing down also involves embracing the beauty of simplicity. This may mean decluttering living spaces, reducing reliance on technology, or finding joy in simple pleasures. By simplifying their environment, families can create a peaceful and nurturing atmosphere that fosters connection and creativity. Embracing simplicity encourages families to focus on what truly matters, fostering a sense of contentment and gratitude.

Nature offers a powerful antidote to the fast pace of modern life. Spending time outdoors, whether in a park, garden, or wilderness, provides an opportunity for families to slow down and connect with the natural world. Nature encourages exploration, curiosity, and wonder, creating a space for families to bond and recharge. Activities such as hiking, picnicking, or stargazing offer moments of serenity and reflection, allowing families to reconnect with themselves and each other.

Cooking and sharing meals together is a timeless tradition that fosters connection and mindfulness. Preparing food as a family encourages collaboration and creativity, while mealtime provides an opportunity for conversation and laughter. By prioritizing shared meals, families create a sense of unity and belonging. This practice also offers a chance to explore cultural traditions, share stories, and express gratitude for the nourishment and companionship.

Balancing structured activities with unstructured playtime is another way to slow down family life. Allowing time for spontaneous play and creativity nurtures imagination and self-expression. It encourages family members to explore their interests and passions in a relaxed and supportive environment. By providing space for unstructured play, families foster a sense of freedom and joy, allowing relationships to flourish.

The practice of gratitude can enrich the experience of slowing down family life. Taking time to express appreciation for one another and for the simple joys of life fosters a positive and compassionate atmosphere. Gratitude rituals, such as sharing what each family member is thankful for at the dinner table, encourage reflection and mindfulness. This practice cultivates a mindset of abundance and contentment, enhancing the quality of family interactions.

Ultimately, slowing down family life is about creating a sanctuary where love, connection, and joy can thrive. It involves making intentional choices that prioritize relationships and well-being over busyness and external pressures. By embracing a slower pace, families cultivate an environment of warmth and togetherness, where each member feels valued and supported. This journey invites families to rediscover the beauty of life in its simplest and most profound moments, creating a legacy of love and connection that will endure for generations.

Community and the Joy of Togetherness

The concept of community is a timeless one, deeply rooted in our human experience. Throughout history, people have sought the company of others, drawn together by shared interests, goals, and values. Community provides a sense of belonging and purpose, offering support and connection that enrich our lives. The joy of togetherness lies in the relationships we build and the collective experiences we share, creating a tapestry of connections that enhance our individual and collective well-being.

Building a strong community begins with the recognition of commonality. It involves identifying shared interests and values that unite individuals, fostering a sense of belonging and mutual understanding. This sense of commonality serves as the foundation upon which relationships are built, encouraging individuals to come together in pursuit of common goals. Whether through shared hobbies, cultural traditions, or social causes, the recognition of common interests fosters a sense of unity and connection.

Engaging with a community involves active participation and contribution. It requires individuals to step beyond their personal sphere and engage with others, offering their skills, knowledge, and support. This active engagement strengthens the fabric of the community, creating a network of support and collaboration. By contributing to the community, individuals enrich their own lives and the lives of others, creating a sense of fulfillment and purpose.

The joy of togetherness is often found in the shared experiences and memories that communities create. Whether participating in a local festival, volunteering for a common cause, or simply gathering for a communal meal, these shared moments foster a sense of connection and belonging. They create memories that are cherished and celebrated, strengthening the bonds between community members. These experiences serve as a reminder of the power of collective action and the joy that comes from being part of something larger than oneself.

Communication plays a vital role in building and sustaining a community. Open and honest communication fosters trust and understanding, encouraging individuals to share their thoughts, ideas, and concerns. This dialogue creates a sense of transparency and inclusion, ensuring that all voices are heard and valued. By prioritizing communication, communities can navigate challenges and conflicts with resilience and grace, strengthening their collective bonds.

Inclusivity is a cornerstone of a thriving community. It involves recognizing and valuing the diverse perspectives and experiences that each member brings. By embracing inclusivity, communities create an environment where all individuals feel welcome and respected, fostering a sense of belonging and acceptance. This inclusivity enriches the community, bringing a wealth of ideas and experiences that enhance the collective experience.

Community events and gatherings serve as a catalyst for connection and engagement. They provide opportunities for individuals to come together, share experiences, and celebrate their shared identity. These events foster a sense of joy and camaraderie, creating a vibrant and dynamic community atmosphere. By participating in community events, individuals strengthen their connections with others, enhancing their sense of belonging and togetherness.

The support and encouragement found within a community are invaluable. Whether through times of celebration or challenge, the presence of a supportive community provides comfort and reassurance. This support fosters resilience, enabling individuals to navigate life's ups and downs with confidence and grace. The knowledge that one is not alone, that there is a network of individuals who care and support one another, is a source of strength and joy.

Intergenerational connections within a community offer a unique and enriching dynamic. The sharing of wisdom, experiences, and traditions between different generations fosters a sense of continuity and legacy. These connections create opportunities for learning and growth, enhancing the well-being of both young and old. By embracing intergenerational relationships, communities create a rich and diverse tapestry of experiences and perspectives.

In a world where technology often replaces face-to-face interactions, the significance of physical community spaces cannot be understated. Parks, community centers, and local cafes serve as gathering places where individuals can connect and engage. These spaces provide a sense of place and belonging, fostering a sense of community identity and pride. By prioritizing the creation and maintenance of community spaces, communities can enhance their sense of togetherness and connection.

The power of storytelling within a community is profound. Sharing personal stories and experiences creates a sense of connection and empathy, allowing individuals to relate to one another on a deeper level. Storytelling fosters understanding and compassion, bridging gaps and building relationships. By embracing storytelling, communities create a rich narrative tapestry that celebrates their shared identity and experiences.

Celebrating the achievements and milestones of community members fosters a sense of pride and joy. Recognizing the accomplishments and contributions of individuals reinforces the values and goals of the community, creating a positive and uplifting atmosphere. These celebrations serve as a reminder of the strength and potential of the community, inspiring individuals to continue contributing and engaging.

Ultimately, the joy of togetherness found within a community enriches our lives in countless ways. It provides a sense of belonging and purpose, offering support and connection that enhances our well-being. By building and nurturing communities, we create a network of relationships that sustain us through life's journey, bringing joy, fulfillment, and meaning. The journey of community building is ongoing, marked by moments of connection, celebration, and growth. Through this journey, we discover the beauty and power of human connection, creating a world where individuals feel seen, heard, and valued.

Chapter 5: Creativity and Personal Expression

Discovering the Joy of Creative Pursuits

Creativity is a fundamental aspect of human nature, a vibrant force that fuels innovation, self-expression, and joy. Engaging in creative pursuits allows individuals to explore their imaginations, express their thoughts and emotions, and connect with the world in unique and meaningful ways. Whether through art, music, writing, or any other form of creative expression, the journey of creativity offers endless opportunities for discovery, growth, and fulfillment.

The joy of creative pursuits begins with the freedom to explore and experiment without the constraints of judgment or expectation. This sense of freedom encourages individuals to venture into the unknown, to take risks and embrace the unexpected. Creativity thrives in an environment where mistakes are seen as opportunities for learning and growth, rather than failures. By letting go of the need for perfection, individuals can open themselves to the joy and spontaneity of the creative process.

An essential aspect of discovering the joy of creative pursuits is finding inspiration. Inspiration can come from a multitude of sources, whether it be nature, personal experiences, or the work of other artists. It serves as the spark that ignites the creative flame, providing ideas and motivation to begin the creative journey. By actively seeking out inspiration, individuals can nurture their creativity and maintain a sense of excitement and curiosity in their pursuits.

Creative pursuits often involve the exploration of diverse mediums and techniques. This exploration allows individuals to discover the tools and methods that resonate most with their unique style and vision. Whether experimenting with watercolors, learning a musical instrument, or writing poetry, trying new things can reveal untapped talents and interests. By embracing a spirit of exploration, individuals can find joy in the process of discovering and honing their creative abilities.

Community plays a vital role in the creative journey, offering support, feedback, and collaboration. Engaging with other creatives provides opportunities for learning and growth, as well as the chance to share ideas and experiences. Creative communities, whether local or online, foster a sense of belonging and connection, encouraging individuals to pursue their passions with confidence and enthusiasm. By participating in a community, individuals can find inspiration and motivation in the shared pursuit of creativity.

The act of creation itself is a powerful form of self-expression, allowing individuals to communicate their thoughts, emotions, and experiences in a tangible and meaningful way. Creative pursuits provide an outlet for processing and understanding the complexities of life, offering clarity and insight. Through creation, individuals can explore their identities and connect with their innermost selves, finding a sense of purpose and fulfillment in the process.

Finding the time and space for creativity is essential for nurturing creative pursuits. In a world filled with distractions and demands, carving out dedicated time for creative expression can be challenging. However, prioritizing creativity as an integral part of daily life fosters a sense of balance and well-being. Creating a physical space that inspires and supports creative work, whether it be a studio, a corner of a room, or a portable setup, can also enhance the creative experience, providing a sanctuary for exploration and expression.

The journey of creativity is often accompanied by periods of self-doubt and uncertainty. These moments are a natural part of the creative process, offering opportunities for reflection and growth. By embracing these challenges with resilience and an open mind, individuals can overcome obstacles and continue to develop their creative abilities. The joy of creative pursuits lies not only in the finished work but in the journey itself, with all its twists and turns.

Creative pursuits offer a unique opportunity to connect with others, whether through collaboration, sharing work, or engaging in creative communities. This connection fosters empathy, understanding, and appreciation for diverse perspectives and experiences. By sharing creative work, individuals invite others into their world, creating a dialogue that transcends language and culture. These connections enrich the creative process, offering new insights and opportunities for growth.

The impact of creative pursuits extends beyond the individual, influencing and inspiring others in profound ways. Creative work has the power to challenge perceptions, provoke thought, and evoke emotion, contributing to cultural and social change. By embracing their creative potential, individuals can make meaningful contributions to the world, leaving a lasting impact on those around them.

Ultimately, discovering the joy of creative pursuits is a journey of exploration, self-expression, and connection. It invites individuals to embrace their unique talents and perspectives, to find fulfillment in the act of creation, and to share their vision with the world. Through creativity, individuals can discover new facets of themselves, connect with others, and experience the joy and wonder of the creative process. As the journey unfolds, creativity becomes a source of inspiration and joy, enriching lives and transforming the world in beautiful and unexpected ways.

The Role of Play and Experimentation

Play and experimentation are essential components of personal development, creativity, and innovation. They are not merely activities for children but are vital processes that enrich our lives, stimulate our minds, and foster growth at any age. Embracing play and experimentation can unlock new potentials, providing opportunities to explore the world in a way that is both joyful and insightful. Through these activities, individuals can tap into their innate curiosity, challenge their limits, and discover new paths of growth and fulfillment.

The essence of play lies in its spontaneity and freedom. It is an activity that is undertaken for its own sake, free from the constraints of judgment, goals, or outcomes. This freedom creates a space for exploration and discovery, where individuals can engage with their environment, ideas, and emotions in a relaxed and open manner. Play encourages a sense of wonder and curiosity, inviting individuals to question, imagine, and dream without limitations.

Experimentation, closely related to play, involves testing and exploring new ideas, methods, or activities. It is a process of trial and error that encourages learning through experience. By experimenting, individuals can break free from conventional thinking, challenge their assumptions, and explore new possibilities. This process fosters a mindset of innovation and adaptability, enabling individuals to navigate change and uncertainty with confidence and creativity.

The role of play and experimentation in fostering creativity cannot be overstated. These activities provide a fertile ground for the imagination to flourish, offering opportunities to explore different perspectives and ideas. In the realm of play, individuals can experiment with new concepts, combine seemingly unrelated elements, and discover novel solutions to problems. This creative exploration fuels innovation, providing the inspiration and insights needed to bring new ideas to life.

Incorporating play and experimentation into daily life can enhance problem-solving skills and critical thinking. By engaging in activities that challenge the mind and encourage exploration, individuals develop the ability to approach problems from multiple angles and consider alternative solutions. This flexibility and open-mindedness are essential for effective problem-solving, enabling individuals to adapt to changing circumstances and find creative solutions to complex challenges.

Play and experimentation also foster resilience and perseverance. In the process of experimenting, individuals encounter failures and setbacks, which are integral to the learning experience. By viewing these challenges as opportunities for growth, individuals build resilience and develop the perseverance needed to overcome obstacles and achieve their goals. This mindset of resilience fosters a sense of confidence and determination, empowering individuals to embrace challenges and pursue their dreams with tenacity.

The social aspect of play and experimentation is equally important. Engaging in these activities with others fosters collaboration, communication, and teamwork. Through play, individuals learn to negotiate, share, and work together towards common goals, building strong social bonds and enhancing interpersonal skills. Experimentation in group settings encourages the exchange of ideas and perspectives, leading to richer and more diverse outcomes. These social interactions not only enhance the experience of play but also contribute to personal and professional growth.

Play and experimentation are powerful tools for emotional and psychological well-being. These activities offer an outlet for self-expression, allowing individuals to explore and process their emotions in a safe and supportive environment. Through play, individuals can experience joy, relaxation, and a sense of accomplishment, all of which contribute to overall well-being. Experimentation encourages self-discovery and personal growth, providing opportunities to explore new interests and passions.

Incorporating play and experimentation into educational and professional settings can enhance learning and performance. In education, play-based learning encourages engagement, motivation, and a deeper understanding of concepts. Experimentation fosters a sense of curiosity and inquiry, encouraging students to explore and apply their knowledge in creative ways. In professional settings, a culture of play and experimentation can lead to increased innovation, collaboration, and job satisfaction, creating a dynamic and productive work environment.

The role of play and experimentation in personal development is profound. These activities encourage individuals to step outside their comfort zones, explore new interests, and discover their unique strengths and talents. By embracing a mindset of play and experimentation, individuals can cultivate a sense of curiosity and openness, leading to continuous growth and self-improvement. This journey of self-discovery is both rewarding and transformative, offering opportunities to explore new facets of oneself and the world.

Play and experimentation can be integrated into daily life in simple yet meaningful ways. Engaging in hobbies, trying new activities, or simply taking time to explore and experiment without a specific goal can enrich one's life and provide a sense of fulfillment and joy. By prioritizing play and experimentation, individuals can create a balanced and harmonious life that nurtures both personal and professional growth.

Ultimately, the role of play and experimentation is to enrich our lives with joy, creativity, and discovery. These activities provide a sense of freedom and exploration, inviting individuals to engage with the world in a way that is both meaningful and fulfilling. Through play and experimentation, we can unlock our full potential, discover new possibilities, and create a life that is rich in experiences and opportunities. This journey of exploration and growth is a celebration of the human spirit, offering endless opportunities for learning, connection, and joy.

Milton Keynes UK
Ingram Content Group UK Ltd.
UKHW021053280824
447551UK00011B/476

9 798330 361212